...world's longest established

Rely on Thomas Cook as your
travelling companion on your next trip
and benefit from our unique heritage.

Thomas Cook **pocket** guides

BATH

Written by Carole French

Published by Thomas Cook Publishing
A division of Thomas Cook Tour Operations Limited
Company registration no. 3772199 England
The Thomas Cook Business Park, Unit 9, Coningsby Road,
Peterborough PE3 8SB, United Kingdom
Email: books@thomascook.com, Tel: +44 (0) 1733 416477
www.thomascookpublishing.com

Produced by Cambridge Publishing Management Limited
Burr Elm Court, Main Street, Caldecote CB23 7NU
www.cambridgepm.co.uk

ISBN: 978-1-84848-466-5

First edition © 2011 Thomas Cook Publishing
Text © Thomas Cook Publishing
Cartography supplied by Redmoor Design, Tavistock, Devon
Map data © OpenStreetMap contributors CC-BY-SA; www.openstreetmap.org,
www.creativecomments.org

Series Editor: Karen Beaulah
Production/DTP: Steven Collins

Printed and bound in Spain by GraphyCems

Cover photography © Thomas Cook Publishing

CONTENTS

SYMBOLS KEY

The following symbols are used throughout this book:

ⓐ address ⓣ telephone ⓕ fax ⓦ website address ⓔ email
ⓛ opening times ⓝ public transport connections ⓘ important

The following symbols are used on the maps:

ⓘ	information office	▣	points of interest
✈	airport	○	city
➕	hospital	○	large town
⬧	police station	○	small town
✉	post office	=	motorway
⊟	bus station	—	main road
➦	railway station	—	minor road
✝	cathedral	—	railway
➊	numbers denote featured cafés, restaurants and venues		

PRICE CATEGORIES

The ratings below indicate average price rates for a double
room per night, including breakfast:

£ under £65 ££ £65–95 £££ £95–125

The typical cost of a three-course meal, without drinks,
is as follows:

£ £10–20 ££ £20–30 £££ £30–40

▶ *Royal Victoria Park overlooked by the Royal Crescent*

INTRODUCING
Bath

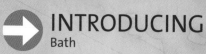

Introduction

From world-famous attractions like the Royal Crescent, a simply breathtaking example of Georgian architecture, to unmatched spa experiences, influential art galleries, the trendiest of restaurants and sophisticated shopping experiences, Bath manages to thrill each and every visitor. Set in the heart of the West Country of England, it has attracted writers, such as Jane Austen and Charles Dickens, painters and sculptors, and is today one of the most popular short-break destinations in Europe.

Bath has enjoyed two golden eras. The first was when the Romans arrived in England in the 1st century AD; they recognised the importance of the city's natural hot springs and went on to make it one of the wealthiest cities in the country. The second was the Georgian period, when one architectural treasure after another was built in what had become a fashionable city and the playground of the aristocracy. These eras make for two distinctive areas of the city, complemented by the serenity of Sydney Gardens and Henrietta Park, which lie just off Great Pulteney Street.

The Roman Baths are in the very heart of the old city. A short walk away is the beautiful abbey, site of an earlier abbey where the first monarch of England, King Edgar, was crowned over 1,000 years ago. Blending in seamlessly is Milsom Street, voted one of the best shopping streets in the country. Nearby, the Circus and Royal Crescent, along with Queen Square and the elegant Assembly Rooms, serve as spectacular reminders of Bath's Georgian era. These and around 5,000 other buildings in the city are listed for their historical importance. To the east of the city is the 18th-century Pulteney Bridge, one of only four bridges in the world with shops built into its original design.

A UNESCO World Heritage Site in its entirety, Bath combines its history with an indisputable modern vibe. The multi-million-pound development of the Holburne Museum of Art, to be unveiled in 2011, is just one project set to enhance the city's cultural edge, while its contemporary award-winning Thermae Bath Spa complex is pure 21st century. Bath is a fun, cosmopolitan city that will capture your heart.

● *The ancient Roman Baths are the city's main tourist attraction*

When to go

SEASONS & CLIMATE

Bath is a city for all seasons. In the spring the parks are ablaze with daffodils and the shops full of new fashions, while the summer months bring opportunities to take boat trips in the sunshine. In winter, Bath takes on a Dickensian feel as Christmas approaches, especially on days that have seen a dusting of snow. The city enjoys a temperate climate. In summer, temperatures peak at around 21°C (70°F), while in spring and autumn they are unlikely to reach more than 10°C (51°F). In winter, temperatures can dip below 0°C (32°F). Bath experiences a slightly higher average rainfall than some areas of England as a result of its close proximity to the Atlantic Ocean.

ANNUAL EVENTS

Bath has a whole host of annual and regular events. The 11-day **Bath Comedy Festival** runs from April Fool's Day (1 April) to 11 April (❶ 01225 463362 ⓦ www.bathcomedyfestival.co.uk ⓔ fun@bathcomedyfestival.co.uk). At the end of May, the ten-day **Bath International Music Festival** attracts classical, jazz and folk musicians from around the world (❶ 01225 462231 ⓦ www.bathmusicfest.org.uk ⓔ info@bathfestivals.org.uk). The **Bath Fringe Festival**, from the end of May to mid-June, includes various performing arts genres (❶ 01225 480079 ⓦ www.bathfringe.co.uk).

    Roman Bath by Torchlight is a popular summer spectacle, which runs from 1 July to 31 August (❶ 01225 477785 ⓦ www.romanbaths.co.uk

ⓔ romanbath_bookings@bathnes.gov.uk). The **Bath Food and Drink Festival** was held for the first time in July 2010 and is set to be an annual event (ⓣ 01242 521997 ⓦ www.garden-events.com).

The ten-day **Bath Festival of Children's Literature**, held at the end of September, attracts top authors (ⓣ 01225 463362 ⓦ www.bathkidslitfest.co.uk ⓔ boxoffice@bathfestivals.org.uk), and the **Jane Austen Festival** is also held in September (ⓣ 01225 443000 ⓦ www.janeausten.co.uk).

The **Bath Film Festival** is a nine-day event held around the middle of November and screens over 40 films (ⓣ 01225 401149 ⓦ www.bathfilmfestival.org.uk). The festive season isn't complete without a visit to the wonderful **Bath Christmas Market**. It runs from the end of November to mid-December (ⓣ 0906 711 2000 ⓦ www.bathchristmasmarket.co.uk).

🔺 *The impressive Georgian Circus*

History

It is said that Bath was founded more than 2,500 years ago when Bladud, the father of King Lear, discovered the springs. It became a place of worship to the ancient Celtic god Sul. When Britain became part of the Roman Empire in around AD 43, Bath enjoyed prosperity. Its thermal baths were legendary. In the 6th century, when the Saxons reigned in the West Country, they founded a monastery that was to become one of the most important in England. It was here in its abbey, the first of three built on the same site, that King Edgar, the first monarch of England, was crowned in AD 973.

The Bishop of Wells took a liking to Bath in the 11th century and built a cathedral on the monastery site, followed by Queen Elizabeth I, whose soirées made it the haunt of the aristocracy. Bath's status culminated in a Royal Charter declaring it a city in 1590. In the late 17th century, Queen Anne developed a penchant for Bath's rejuvenating waters. By this time it was one of the most fashionable spa resorts in England.

Bath's zenith came during this period. In the 1700s, the city was transformed by three men: the distinguished architect John Wood, the entrepreneur Ralph Allen, owner of the stone quarries at Combe Down, and London socialite Richard Nash, who was to become the 'King of Bath' and introduced social reforms. Between 1728 and 1775, John Wood's masterpieces of design, Queen Square, Prior Park, the Circus and the iconic Royal Crescent, were built. John Wood died in 1754, and his son, John Wood the Younger, completed his work. In 1770, a new leading light in architecture, Robert Adam, designed the Pulteney Bridge based on Florence's Ponte Vecchio.

Bath suffered damage during World War II and the need to preserve its heritage became apparent. In 1987, the entire city was declared a UNESCO World Heritage Site. Today, Bath is known for its cultural venues, shopping and chic café society. One of its most recent projects was the Thermae Bath Spa, a multi-million-pound spa centre that has been voted one of the best in the world.

▲ Bath Abbey

Culture

Bath has a long-established cultural heritage. In the 18th and 19th centuries it was a favourite haunt of writers, sculptors and painters. Jane Austen and Charles Dickens wrote many of their great works here, and artist Thomas Gainsborough found inspiration in the city.

It enjoys a pavement café scene and lively cultural events. You could easily combine a morning museum trip, a stop at a bookshop and a spot of lunch with an afternoon admiring great works by Picasso, Matisse or local contemporary artists in one of the many art galleries, followed by an evening at the theatre and a gourmet dinner.

The city has five theatres that regularly attract international performers and directors, and venues for musical theatre, orchestral, operatic and pop performances, and organ recitals. Jazz can be found in smaller venues and you have your pick of piano bars and clubs where bands play indie, garage, R&B and rock. Bath regularly hosts art exhibitions, literature events and fringe theatre festivals, and has even had the starring role as a backdrop in films and television productions.

Indulge in a relaxing visit to the Thermae Bath Spa

MAKING THE MOST OF
Bath

Shopping

Bath is known for its outstanding shops, selling everything from designer fashions and chic accessories to antiques, handmade toys and chocolates.

WHERE TO SHOP

The city has six main shopping districts. Milsom Street, Broad Street and a labyrinth of smaller streets make up the Milsom Quarter. Here you will find fashion labels like Armani and Dolce & Gabbana. For big-name shops like WH Smith and Marks & Spencer, along with specialist shops selling jewellery, gifts, books and confectionery, head for the central area around Union Street. You will also find the entrance to the Guildhall Market here, which is open every day and full of artisans' stalls. Be sure to take the short detour to Pulteney Bridge, one of only four bridges in the world to have shops along its length.

Bath is a paradise for anyone who loves art, antiques and crafts. The little lanes around London Street, known as the Artisan Quarter, have an eclectic mix of specialist shops selling all these goodies and more. Every Saturday there's a flea market here too. The Podium Shopping Centre, created within a period-style building and one of several modern malls in the city, is located here. SouthGate is a shining new shopping district being created to the south of the city, and will be home to all the major department stores; in contrast, the Upper Town district near Royal Crescent has influential art galleries and jewellery shops. The Western Quarter is home to one of Bath's busiest markets, the highly regarded Farmers' Market.

WHAT TO BUY

To say Bath's shopping districts have something for everyone may be a bit of a cliché, but it's entirely true. Here you can find the latest fashions, beautiful ceramics and glassware, works of art and handmade jewellery, along with everything you would expect to find in top-name high-street stores. In the Artisan Quarter's flea market you will find reclaimed antiques and curios, while in the Bath Farmers' Market you will find the freshest of produce and great cakes and cookies that will, without doubt, make their way into your shopping basket.

🔺 *Many of the high-street names are represented at The Podium*

Eating & drinking

Whether you fancy a drink and light snack in the open air or a full à la carte experience in an award-winning restaurant, then you'll find Bath provides a host of options. There are pavement cafés for a quick espresso and salad, and tea rooms for the quintessential afternoon refreshment break. Oriental, French and Italian restaurants offer the finest cuisine from their regions, and if your taste buds crave spicy Mexican or ethnic dishes, something fishy or a quick meal like a hamburger or pizza, then you'll have plenty of choice. Bath also has gastro pubs. Many have their own garden dining areas if you wish to dine alfresco, some are hidden away behind ancient walls, others have views of the river or the parks.

WHERE TO EAT

You can combine sightseeing in the old city centre with enjoying its cafés and restaurants, including the Pump Room, where traditional Bath Buns are served, or Sally Lunn's Refreshment House tucked inside the city's oldest building. Both the Upper Town and the Pulteney Quarter have lots of stylish restaurants, or you could head for the parks, gardens or the riverside for a picnic. If it's a Saturday, why not buy your fresh picnic food at the Bath Farmers' Market at Green Park Station?
📞 01761 490624 Ⓦ www.bathfarmersmarket.co.uk

WHAT TO EAT

Bath has some regional treats you should try. Top of the list has to be the Bath Bun, invented by Dr Oliver, a physician who helped found the city's Royal Mineral Water Hospital in the 18th century. Although the original recipe was rich and full of calories, today's version is less so. It is made with sweet yeast dough, topped with sugar. Dr Oliver also invented crackers, to eat with cheese, that bear his name and are found throughout England. In Bath they are often served with cheese from nearby Cheddar. The Sally Lunn Bun is a city favourite too, and when this airy brioche bun is served with cream and jam or buttered with a savoury topping, it is simply delicious.

⬤ *Sally Lunn's is the oldest house in Bath*

Entertainment

From theatre to cinema, literary events, dance and art, Bath has venues catering for all artistic genres. Add to this some talented street performers and a year-round programme of festivals, and you have a city bursting with ideas for entertainment.

THEATRE, FILM & MUSIC

Bath has five theatres, each with a year-round programme of drama productions, operas, ballet and musical theatre, including the much-respected Theatre Royal Bath (ⓦ www.theatreroyal.org.uk) and its new cutting-edge venue for children, the egg. Film buffs have a choice of two cinemas, one showing the latest blockbusters and the other thematic films for adults and children from around the world. Musical entertainment takes the form of organ recitals in Bath Abbey, pop and classical concerts in the city's new 1,700-seat venue, the Forum, and many private venues where you can catch jazz musicians and local bands playing everything from indie and R&B to rock.

COMEDY, ART & LITERATURE

Bath's comedy scene is eclectic, and along with its theatres that regularly host comedy productions there is a growing number of clubs where international stand-up performers queue to appear. The city's inspiring art galleries offer viewings of paintings and sculptures, and regularly hold special events and exhibitions, while Bath's many excellent new and second-hand bookshops host signing events and readings. Bath is a city of festivals, including the Bath Fringe Festival, the Bath Festival of Children's Literature and the Jane Austen Festival.

WHERE TO BUY TICKETS

All the theatre, film and music venues, other than the privately owned music clubs, have a box office where tickets can be purchased. Most have an online facility too, such as the Theatre Royal Bath (ⓦ www.theatreroyal.org.uk). For small clubs, along with comedy clubs, bookshops and art galleries, call the venue directly. The Bath Tourist Information Centre next to Bath Abbey will assist with booking tickets. For festivals call the Bath Festivals Box Office in Church Street (ⓣ 01225 463362 ⓦ www.bathfestivals.org.uk). For more information on what's on, see page 93.

🔺 *The Pavilion is a great venue for music, dance and exhibitions*

Sport & relaxation

SPECTATOR SPORTS
Football & rugby

The Bath Rugby Club plays a season of fixtures at The Recreation Ground, known locally as The Rec, while Bath City Football Club plays at Twerton Park. Tickets can be purchased at the grounds, or visit the teams' websites to purchase e-tickets online.

Bath Rugby ⓐ 11 Argyle Street ⓣ 01225 325200
ⓦ www.bathrugby.co.uk ⓔ info@bathrugby.com ⓝ Bus: 4

Bath City Football Club ⓐ Twerton Park, Twerton on Avon
ⓦ www.bathcityfc.com ⓝ Bus: 5

Horse racing

The Bath Racecourse has an annual programme of around 20 flat-racing events. All tickets are available from the racecourse booking office or online.

⬥ *Enjoy a day at the races*

Bath Racecourse ⓐ Lansdown Hill ⓣ 01225 424609
ⓦ www.bath-racecourse.co.uk ⓝ A race-day bus service is
provided by First Bus Company (ⓣ 01224 650100
ⓕ 01224 650140 ⓦ www.firstgroup.com) Bus: 22 leaves
Dorchester Street, opposite Bath Spa station

Motor racing

Experience the thrill of watching cars, supercars and
motorcycles race at the Castle Combe Circuit.
Castle Combe Circuit ⓐ Castle Combe, Chippenham
ⓣ 01249 782417 ⓦ www.castlecombecircuit.co.uk

PARTICIPATION SPORTS

Golf

There are two good 18-hole courses within easy reach of Bath
city centre, along with two 18-hole courses at The Park resort.
Bath Golf Club ⓐ Golf Course Road ⓣ 01225 463824
ⓦ www.bathgolfclub.org.uk ⓔ proshop@bathgolfclub.org.uk
Bowood Golf and Country Club ⓐ Bowood ⓣ 01249 822228
ⓦ www.bowood.org ⓔ proshop@bowood.org
The Park Hotel Golf Course ⓐ The Park, Wick ⓣ 0117 937 1783
ⓦ www.theparkresort.com ⓔ info@tpresort.com

Keep fit & roller-skating

The Bath Pavilion has dance and keep-fit classes, and roller-
skating. Tickets direct from the venue or pay on entry.
Bath Pavilion ⓐ North Parade Road ⓣ 01225 486902
ⓦ www.bathpavilion.org ⓔ info@bathpavilion.org ⓛ Variable
ⓝ Bus: 4

Accommodation

Whether it's a luxury hotel and spa complex, a family-oriented resort, or a cosy B&B that you favour, the city has a range to suit. Booking accommodation in the city centre, around the Circus area and near Pulteney Bridge, ensures the main sights of Bath are within easy walking distance. Out-of-town establishments can be quieter, and with Bath's good transport network it is possible to get into the centre easily. Making a reservation is straightforward, either via the Bath Tourism website (ⓦ www.visitbath.co.uk) or direct with the establishment. It is advisable to book ahead of your stay if possible, since rooms can fill up many months in advance, especially at festival times.

Rooms are regularly inspected by the tourist board or similar authorities like the AA and are awarded a star rating based on quality and services. For example, an establishment with five stars will offer luxurious surroundings and amenities, while establishments awarded one or two stars will generally have fewer amenities, but maintain a good level of cleanliness and basic facilities. If an establishment is unrated, it is generally not recommended by the local tourist board.

CITY CENTRE

Anabelle's Guesthouse £ This newly refurbished bed and breakfast guesthouse offers contemporary rooms and suites, and a central location. ⓐ 6 Manvers Street ⓣ 01225 330133 ⓦ www.anabellesguesthouse.co.uk ⓔ info@anabellesguesthouse.co.uk ⓝ Central city bus service

Harington's Hotel £–££ Located in a pretty cobbled side street, this boutique hotel has stylish guestrooms and a café-bar. ⓐ Queen Street ⓣ 01225 461728 ⓦ www.haringtonshotel.co.uk ⓔ post@haringtonshotel.co.uk ⓝ Central city bus service

Three Abbey Green ££ This stylish hotel is housed in a 17th-century Grade 2 listed town house on one of Bath's prettiest squares.
ⓐ 3 Abbey Green ⓣ 01225 428558 ⓦ www.threeabbeygreen.com ⓔ stay@threeabbeygreen.com ⓝ Central city bus service

Royal Hotel ££–£££ A stylish Victorian hotel in the centre of Bath, the Royal offers a range of accommodation options and features, including dining à la carte. ⓐ Manvers Street ⓣ 0844 5449246 ⓦ www.royalhotelbath.co.uk ⓔ info@royalhotelbath.co.uk ⓝ Central city bus service

Hilton Bath City £££ This de-luxe hotel offers views of the river and fine cuisine in its Mediterranean-style restaurant. ⓐ Walcot Street ⓣ 01225 463411 ⓦ www.hilton.co.uk ⓔ info@hilton.co.uk ⓝ Bus: 6, 7, 13, 231, 232, 271, 272, 273

UPPER TOWN
Bay Tree House £ Refinements include Egyptian linen and the proprietor-cum-chef's special breakfast at this smart guesthouse minutes from Royal Crescent. ⓐ 12 Crescent Gardens ⓣ 01225 483699 ⓦ www.baytreehousebath.co.uk ⓔ stay@baytreehousebath.co.uk ⓝ Bus: 2, 6

Brooks Guesthouse £–££ Organic and free-range ingredients are on the menu at this award-winning bed and breakfast guesthouse. Ⓐ 1 Crescent Gardens, Upper Bristol Road Ⓣ 01225 425543 Ⓦ www.brooksguesthouse.com Ⓔ info@brooksguesthouse.com Ⓝ Bus: 2, 6

Royal Park Guest House ££ This elegant guesthouse offers a relaxing base and is minutes from the Upper Town's sights. Ⓐ 16 Crescent Garden Ⓣ 01225 317651 Ⓦ www.royalparkbath.co.uk Ⓔ info@royalparkbath.co.uk Ⓝ Bus: 2, 6

The Queensberry Hotel £££ Celebrating British traditions, this hotel offers elegant guest rooms and its super Olive Tree restaurant. Ⓐ Russell Street Ⓣ 01225 447928 Ⓦ www.thequeensbery.co.uk Ⓔ reservations@thequeensberry.co.uk Ⓝ Bus: 2, 6

Royal Crescent Hotel £££ Housed in one of Bath's beautiful 18th-century houses, this hotel offers fine dining and a luxurious spa complex. Ⓐ 16 Royal Crescent Ⓣ 01225 823333 Ⓦ www.royalcrescent.co.uk Ⓔ info@royalcrescent.co.uk Ⓝ Bus: 2, 6

PULTENEY QUARTER
Edgar Townhouse £–££ This tastefully presented bed and breakfast hotel offers a base in one of Bath's most fashionable thoroughfares. Ⓐ 64 Great Pulteney Street Ⓣ 01225 420619 Ⓦ www.edgar-townhouse.co.uk Ⓔ stay@edgar-townhouse.co.uk Ⓝ Bus: 8, 18, 264, 265, 418, 419

Bathwick Townhouse ££ Original Georgian architecture features in the Bathwick's two self-contained guest suites. ⓐ 15 Daniel Street ⓣ 01225 420499 ⓦ www.thebathwicktownhouse.com ⓔ justine@thebathwicktownhouse.com ⓝ Bus: 8, 18, 418, 419

Dukes Hotel £££ This super Palladian-style hotel offers period luxury. Dining is on the garden terrace. ⓐ Great Pulteney Street ⓣ 01225 787960 ⓦ www.dukesbath.co.uk ⓔ info@dukesbath.co.uk ⓝ Bus: 8, 18, 264, 265, 418, 419

Macdonald Bath Spa Hotel £££ With a butler service, spa suite and luxurious décor, a stay at this mansion hotel should be memorable. ⓐ Sydney Road ⓣ 01225 444424 ⓦ www.macdonaldhotels.co.uk ⓔ reservations@macdonaldhotels.co.uk ⓝ Bus: 4, 8, 18, 264, 265

OUT OF TOWN

Aquae Sulis £–££ A Victorian hotel located a leisurely riverside walk away from the centre of Bath, the Aquae Sulis is newly refurbished. ⓐ 174/176 Newbridge Road ⓣ 01225 420061 ⓦ www.aquaesulishotel.co.uk ⓔ enquiries@aquaesulishotel.co.uk ⓝ Bus: 337, 339, 418, X39

Barcelo Combe Grove Manor Hotel £££ Offering sports and leisure amenities, such as a gymnasium and tennis, this country club lies around 3km (1¾ miles) from the city. ⓐ Brassknocker Hill, Monkton Combe ⓣ 01225 834644 ⓦ www.combegrovemanor.com ⓔ enquiries@coombegrovemanor.com ⓝ Bus: 1

THE BEST OF BATH

Bath has such a wonderful collection of Roman, Georgian and cosmopolitan treasures that to the first-time visitor it may all seem a little overwhelming. The key is to head for the main sights first and, of course, to take time to experience the gloriously warm spa waters that made Bath famous. The city is a foodies' paradise, so fit in some fine dining and a Bath Bun snack, but above all take time to wander at a leisurely pace and enjoy Bath's cultural attractions.

TOP 10 ATTRACTIONS

- **Royal Crescent** It's the iconic image of Bath and even if you are not an architectural buff its sheer beauty is thrilling (see page 58).

- **The Circus** Just how John Wood the Elder created this design masterpiece will leave you bewildered (see page 57).

- **Jane Austen Centre** We have Ms Austen to thank for classics like *Pride and Prejudice*; this centre tells her story (see pages 60–61).

- **Theatre Royal** Catch a comedy or drama performance at this beautiful old theatre (see page 46).

- **Bath Abbey** Visit the abbey site and imagine how life was when the first king of England was crowned here (see page 44).

- **Hot-Air Balloon Trip** Seeing Bath from the air is a memory that will last a lifetime (see page 29).

- **Pump Room** Once the party venue of gentry and now a great place to enjoy a Bath Bun (see page 49).

- **Roman and Thermae Baths** Experience the waters at the ancient or modern baths (see pages 45 & 46–7).

- **Pulteney Bridge** Admire the sheer beauty of this bridge from the vantage point of a river boat (see page 70).

- **Shopping** No visit to Bath would be complete without a trip around its fabulous shopping streets (see pages 14, 50, 63 & 73).

⬇ *Cure your ailments at the Pump Room fountain*

Suggested itineraries

HALF DAY: BATH IN A HURRY

Head for Royal Crescent, which really shouldn't be missed. Be sure to see inside No 1 Royal Crescent. It has been restored and furnished as it would have been by a wealthy family living in the 1780s. Take the short walk along Brock Street to the Circus, another striking example of Georgian architecture. From here, take a ten-minute walk along Gay Street to the city centre and look out for the signs to the Roman Baths. This complex is regarded as one of the finest ancient spas in the world and is the only source of hot spring water in England.

1 DAY: TIME TO SEE A LITTLE MORE

The half-day itinerary above could easily stretch into a full day. A short walk from the Roman Baths is Bath Abbey, a beautiful example of religious architecture and considered the last of the country's greatest medieval churches. Underneath the abbey is the Bath Abbey Heritage Vaults, a great museum. Now take the short walk along Grand Parade to see Pulteney Bridge, one of only four bridges in the world with shops built into the original 18th-century design.

2–3 DAYS: SHORT CITY-BREAK

Over two or three days you could enjoy all the above sights and see other places of interest as you stroll. For example, on your walk from the Circus to the Roman Baths you will pass by the Jane Austen Centre, which celebrates the life and work of this great author, and the Theatre Royal, one of the oldest theatres in the country. Next to the Roman Baths is the Pump Room, once a fashionable meeting place for the aristocracy and now a fine dining restaurant, and the ultra-modern Thermae Bath Spa complex.

LONGER: ENJOYING BATH TO THE FULL

If you have more time, try taking a hot-air balloon trip over the city (visit ⓦ www.visitbath.co.uk for more information) or a boat trip on the River Avon or the Kennet and Avon Canal. You could visit the Fashion Museum, Henrietta Park, Sydney Gardens and the Holburne Museum of Art, or go a little out of town to the American Museum.

◐ Take a boat trip along the River Avon

Something for nothing

A great way to see Bath is on foot. Strolling along its main streets will reveal little hidden alleys and courtyards, some cobbled and lined with intriguing antique or craft shops. Many have appeared in films and if you visit the tourist board's website (ⓦ www.visitbath.co.uk) you can download a free movie map. *Vanity Fair* (2004) and *The Duchess* (2007) were set here.

You can sip the spring water in the Spa Visitor Centre, visit the Victoria Art Gallery or the Assembly Rooms to see where the gentry of 18th-century England danced and played. Admission is free when the venue is not in use for functions. On a fine summer's day head for Henrietta Park or Sydney Gardens and enjoy the landscaped lawns, or window-shop in Bath's wonderful shops.

JANE AUSTEN (1775–1817)

Jane Austen famously lived in Bath from 1800 to 1809. Although two of her most famous novels are set in Bath, *Northanger Abbey* and *Persuasion* (both published posthumously in 1817), her time in Bath was not very productive. Her literary success only began after moving to her brother Edward's house in Chawton in Hampshire.

The tourist board offers a free MP3 download and a map of a walking tour called *In the footsteps of Jane Austen*. It features extracts from her works and guides you past the places where she lived as well as the sights as they would have been in Georgian times.

When it rains

Whether you adore fashion, history or art, there's plenty to see in Bath's museums and galleries. Learn about Jane Austen and life in Georgian and Regency England at the Jane Austen Centre and see how a wealthy 18th-century family lived at No 1 Royal Crescent Museum.

The Fashion Museum has a magnificent collection of costumes dating as far back as the 16th century, and gives a fascinating look at how fashion has changed up to the modern day. The Holburne Museum has an extensive display of period and modern decorative art, while the city's art galleries have works by local and international artists. To find out about how Bath was created, head for the Building of Bath Collection. It is housed in a Gothic chapel.

You could spend a couple of hours inside Bath Abbey and its Heritage Vaults, and even climb the 212 steps of the tower for a view of the city, but take an umbrella. For a relaxing treat take the waters at the Thermae Bath Spa or one of Bath's smaller spa centres dotted around the city.

On arrival

ARRIVING

By air

The city is served by **Bristol International Airport**
(🅦 www.bristolairport.co.uk), which is around 30 km (20 miles)
from Bath. The airport has all the services you would expect of
a major regional hub, including foreign exchange and ATMs,
tourist information and car hire. International flights also arrive
into London's Heathrow Airport (🅦 www.heathrowairport.com)
and Gatwick Airport (🅦 www.gatwickairport.com), which are
around 160 km (100 miles) and 225 km (140 miles) away from
Bath respectively. All are linked to Bath via road, express coach
and rail networks.

From the airport: Bristol International Flyer express coaches
leave from outside Bristol International Airport's terminal every
15 minutes for Bristol Temple Meads train station. From there
take the train to Bath Spa station. The coach service operates
daily from 03.05 to 23.45. Allow around 60 minutes from the
airport to Bath. You can purchase a combined ticket for the
Bristol International Flyer and the onward train journey to
Bath in advance from around £10. Book online at
🅦 www.thetrainline.com or 🅦 www.fgwtickets.co.uk. Tickets
can also be purchased on board for the journey and at
Bristol station for onward train travel to Bath.

Taxis are available from outside Bristol International Airport
and are generally metered. You can also negotiate a fixed price.
Alternatively, book ahead for an often cheaper
fixed price that will include any waiting time and parking. Allow

around £50 per journey. The journey time is likely to be around 40 minutes. There are many taxi companies to choose from, including Bristol Airport Chauffeurs (ⓦ www.bristolairportchauffeurs.com) and Style Taxis (ⓦ www.styletaxis.co.uk).

Bristol International Airport has a car-hire centre located in the short-stay car park. Vehicles from major companies such as Europcar, Avis and Hertz can be booked, collected if booked in advance, and returned. The journey to Bath is straightforward. Follow the road signs for the A38 towards Bristol, and once on the A38 look out for the A4174 ring road signposted to Bath. Follow the signs for the A4 to Bath, and then the A36/A367 to the city centre.

By rail

The main city-centre rail station is Bath Spa station, located off Dorchester Street near the new SouthGate Shopping Centre. Trains arrive direct from London Paddington station and London Waterloo station, each with a journey time of around 90 minutes. The price for a return ticket is from around £19. Look out for special offers by operator First Great Western.

You can also get to Bath Spa station from stations such as Cardiff Central, Portsmouth Harbour, Frome, Gloucester, Southampton and Brighton, along with trains from destinations throughout the rest of the UK via Bristol Temple Meads.

By bus & coach

National Express (ⓦ www.nationalexpress.com) coaches operate from London Victoria coach station with a journey time of

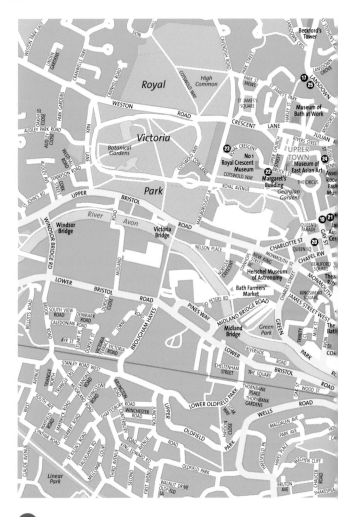

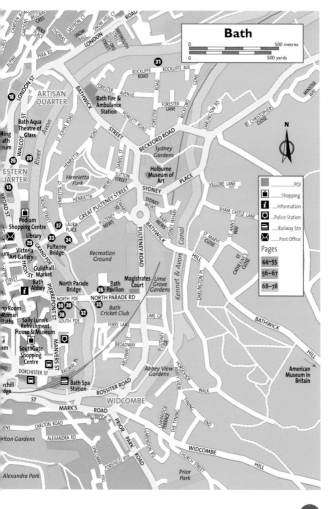

around three and a half hours, and from London Heathrow and London Gatwick airports into Bath city centre. Journey times from the airports average around two and a half hours. Prices are from around £28 and are bookable online.

By car
Bath is best approached via Junction 18 on the M4 motorway from London and Wales, which links from the M5 motorway from Devon and Cornwall. Follow the A46 signposted to Bath, turning off onto the A4, which runs straight into the city centre via the A36/A367. Take care around Milsom Street and Grand Parade where some streets are one-way.

FINDING YOUR FEET
The city centre is easy to navigate, but be sure to find a good map. You can download a map from the Bath Tourism website (ⓦ www.visitbath.co.uk) or purchase one from garages, bookshops or newsagents. Like all cities, Bath is a busy place and minor crime like pickpocketing does exist, so it is wise to be vigilant.

ORIENTATION
The River Avon runs from the north of the city to the west, enclosing Bath in a semicircular fashion. The city centre and the Upper Town district lie within the semicircle, while the Pulteney Quarter lies across the river to the east. A good landmark if you are exploring the city centre is Bath Abbey. Its tower dominates the skyline. Across the Abbey Churchyard are the Roman Baths and the Pump Room, while minutes away are

Thermae Bath Spa, Abbey Green and Sally Lunn's Refreshment House and Museum.

The added bonus of making the abbey your landmark is that the Bath Tourist Information Centre is housed in the Abbey Chambers next door. Bath Abbey and the Abbey Churchyard are within easy reach of the main shopping areas around Milsom Street too. If you start with the abbey behind you and facing Orange Grove and the river, to get there turn left and walk along the High Street. Look out for the Guildhall on your right. Cross over the Bridge Street junction and turn into New Bond Street, which will take you through to Milsom Street.

At the far end of Milsom Street is George Street. If you turn left here and then right into Gay Street you will approach the Circus. If you are planning to explore the Upper Town district

⬤ *Bath Spa station is a Grade II* listed building*

then the Circus is the best landmark from which to get your bearings. From here you can see Royal Crescent at the far end of Brock Street, the Museum of East Asian Art and the Fashion Museum, the Assembly Rooms and the Building of Bath Collection. Once you have explored this district, retrace your steps back to the Circus, George Street, Milsom Street and to the Bridge Street junction, and you can turn left towards the river and head over the beautiful Pulteney Bridge. In turn, the bridge will take you to Great Pulteney Street, the Holburne Museum of Art and the glorious parklands of Sydney Gardens and Henrietta Park in the Pulteney Quarter.

GETTING AROUND

Most of the sights in the city centre, Upper Town and the Pulteney Quarter are best seen on foot, but there is a good bus network that links one side of the city with the other, and all places of interest.

By bus

Buses in and around Bath are operated by the First Group (📞 01224 650100 🌐 www.firstgroup.com) with all bus routes leaving from the bus station on Dorchester Street opposite the Bath Spa train station. A route map and timetable are available from the station's information point. Zone 1 covers the areas of the city centre, as well as part of the Upper Town and the Pulteney Quarter, with Zone 2 circling and covering areas out as far as the University of Bath, Beacon Hill and Lower Weston. Zone 3 forms the outer circle and covers Claverton Down, Combe Down and Twerton, Upper Weston and Fairfield Park.

Among the routes are services 8 and 18 that serve the university, service 2 for Lansdown Road, services 1 and 13 that serve Combe Down and a central bus service for the city centre. A special race-day bus service is provided by First Bus Company to Bath Racecourse. It leaves Dorchester Street two hours before the start of the first race, and thereafter at half-hour intervals. Attractions and towns around Bath are well served by the bus

🔺 Bath's historic buildings display beautiful architectural detail

network, so if you are planning a trip to Bradford on Avon on the edge of the Cotswolds, for instance, take service 264/265. The beautiful Prior Park is served by service 2, the cathedral city of Wells by service 173, Lacock village by service 231/233 and Bristol by service X39.

Bath's taxi companies offer short- or long-distance trips. The main taxi ranks can be found outside the Bath Spa train and bus stations, at Westgate Buildings, which is a short walk from the Theatre Royal, and next to Bath Abbey off Orange Grove.

Car hire

Hiring a car from a local or national company and driving around Bath, or to nearby places of interest, is relatively straightforward, providing you have all the correct documentation. There are plenty of garages for fuel, and although Bath has limited off-street parking there are 12 signposted long- and short-stay car parks and four Park & Ride sites. There are designated parking bays in most of the city's car parks and in some streets for disabled drivers (see pages 92–3).

❶ *Pulteney Bridge has shops along both sides, an architectural rarity*

THE CITY OF
Bath

Introduction

The three areas of Bath covered in the next chapters each have their own distinct characters and attractions. Whether you adore leisurely picnics in large open parklands, riverside walks, cobbled alleys or fabulous architecture, each area will give you lots of opportunities to indulge your passions.

In the city centre chapter we cover the area bordered by Manvers Street and Pierrepont Street to the east, up the High Street and Broad Street, George Street to the north and down to the river along Gay Street and Charles Street to Dorchester Street. Within these parameters there is the glorious Bath Abbey, the Roman Baths and plenty of other sights.

In the Upper Town chapter we head beyond the elegant Queen Square, north along Gay Street to the Circus. This is the area of the Royal Crescent and Assembly Rooms, museums and the huge Royal Victoria Park.

In our final chapter we visit the Pulteney Quarter, home to the enchanting Pulteney Bridge, the Holburne Museum of Art, and the parks and recreational grounds that lie to the east of the city centre.

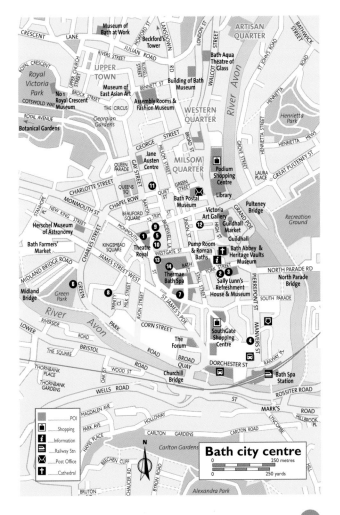

Bath city centre

0 — 250 metres
0 — 250 yards

POI
Shopping
Information
Railway Stn
Post Office
Cathedral

City centre

The combination of ancient buildings that blend in harmony with modern structures like the Thermae Bath Spa complex gives the city centre a sense of drama. Add designer fashion shops and trendy restaurants and you have a vibrant area of Bath.

SIGHTS & ATTRACTIONS

Bath Abbey

The beautiful medieval Abbey Church of Saint Peter and Saint Paul, commonly known as Bath Abbey, is a landmark of the city. It is the third to have stood on this site. The first dated from 757; the first king of England, King Edgar, was crowned here in 973. Services have been held in the abbey for over a thousand years. It is possible to take a 45-minute guided tour every day except Sundays. See its Gothic architecture, spectacular vaulted ceilings and bells, and climb the 212 steps to the top of the tower for a panoramic view of the city. ⓐ Abbey Churchyard ⓣ 01225 422462 ⓦ www.bathabbey.org ⓔ office@bathabbey.org ⓛ 09.00–18.00 Mon–Sat, 13.00–14.30 Sun (summer); 09.00–16.30 Mon–Sat, 13.00–14.30 Sun (winter) ⓝ Central city bus service ⓘ Admission charge to tower

Guildhall

An imposing Grade I listed building, the Guildhall dates from the late 18th century. It was built to the designs of prominent Bath architect Thomas Warr Attwood. Made of honey-coloured Bath stone, it features Ionic-style columns and intricate detailing to its façade, and a huge banqueting hall inside used for official functions, weddings and special festival events, which you can see on a visit. Its Georgian architecture is well worth seeing. Its offices are used by the local council. ⓐ High Street ⓕ 01225 477724 ⓦ www.bathvenues.co.uk ⓛ 09.00–17.00 Mon–Fri ⓝ Central city bus service

Roman Baths

Dating back 2,000 years, the Roman Baths lie at the source of England's only hot spring. You can take a tour to see the Sacred Spring where the water reaches temperatures of 46°C (114°F), the Roman Temple where the goddess Sulis Minerva was worshipped, the Great Bath and a display of archaeological finds from the site at below ground level, and the Georgian Pump Room above. During the summer months, personnel dressed in

ⓞ *Bath's beautiful Guildhall is a popular wedding venue*

Roman costumes give visits a nice touch, and there are audio guides available in eight languages. ⓐ Abbey Churchyard ⓣ 01225 477785 ⓦ www.romanbaths.co.uk ⓔ romanbaths_bookings@bathnes.gov.uk ⓛ 09.00–21.00 daily (summer); 09.00–17.00 daily (spring and autumn); 09.30–16.30 daily (winter). Roman Baths by Torchlight until 22.00 daily, July–Aug only ⓝ Central city bus service ⓘ Admission charge

Theatre Royal

One of the oldest theatres in England, and a Grade II* listed building because of its outstanding Georgian architecture, the Theatre Royal was built around 1720 and features a lavish red and gold tiered auditorium with a *trompe l'œil* ceiling. It offers a programme of drama and comedy performances, musical concerts, ballet and opera throughout the year. Just behind the theatre is the Ustinov studio, where contemporary drama and comedy shows are performed, and its innovative children's theatre, the egg. On site is an à la carte restaurant and a family café. It has good facilities for visitors with limited mobility, impaired hearing and sight. ⓐ Saw Close ⓣ 01225 448844 ⓦ www.theatreroyal.org.uk ⓔ enquiries@theatreroyal.org.uk ⓛ Variable, please check before visiting ⓝ Central city bus service ⓘ Admission charge for performances

Thermae Bath Spa

The city's contemporary new spa centre offers the chance to relax in pools fed by the warm mineral-rich spring waters. Enjoy the Minerva Bath with massage jets, the open-air rooftop pool and steam rooms. Within the complex is a treatment suite where body wraps, massage and facials are among the menu items, while the Spa Visitor Centre has an interesting narrative on the history of Bath's spa from Roman times to the present day. There's a café and a shop offering lots of lovely-smelling spa products. ⓐ Hot Bath Street ⓣ 0844 888 0844 ⓦ www.thermaebathspa.com ⓔ info@thermaebathspa.com ⓛ 09.00–22.00 daily ⓝ Central city bus service ❶ Admission charge to use spa and for treatments

CULTURE

Bath Abbey Heritage Vaults Museum

Spend some time in this fascinating museum created in the restored 18th-century cellars under the pavement on the south side of Bath Abbey. The museum guides the visitor through periods of history that saw different buildings standing on the abbey site, and explains how they were designed and constructed. There are beautifully preserved statues, sculptures and artefacts from the present abbey and the previous abbeys that stood on the site, which are carefully arranged and lit with atmospheric lighting. Some statues and items date from Saxon times. An information board and voiceover explain what each piece is and how it might have been used. ⓐ Abbey Churchyard ⓣ 01225 303314 ⓦ www.bathabbey.org ⓔ office@bathabbey.org ⓛ 10.00–17.00 Mon–Sat, closed Sun

Bath Postal Museum

This interesting museum tells the story of the United Kingdom's postal system, including how the first adhesive stamp, the

Penny Black, was posted in Broad Street, Bath, on 2 May 1840.
You can discover what life was like on a Victorian Mail Coach,
the history of postboxes and how the mail has been delivered
over the centuries. Exhibits include stamp collections, postboxes from different decades and a replica of an early Victorian
postbox. Themed narratives trace the history of writing letters,
and there are displays of paper, quills and ink. ⓐ 27 Northgate
Street ⓞ 01225 460333 ⓦ www.bathpostalmuseum.org
ⓔ info@bathpostalmuseum.org ⓛ 11.00–17.00 Mon–Sat
(summer); 11.00–16.30 (winter), closed Sun ⓝ Central city bus
service ⓘ Admission charge

Herschel Museum of Astronomy

This museum is dedicated to the life and work of William
Herschel (1738–1822), who has been described by Sir Patrick

⬤ Bath is a compact city and easy to navigate

Moore, the astronomer best known for his television work and patron of the museum, as the finest telescope maker of his time; it occupies Herschel's former home. It was here that he observed and furthered our understanding of the solar system, and discovered the planet Uranus in 1781 using his own telescope. Exhibits include a replica of the telescope, rooms and a workshop presented as it would have been when Herschel used it in the 18th century. **ⓐ** 19 New King Street **ⓣ** 01225 446865 **ⓦ** www.bath-preservation-trust.org.uk **ⓔ** admin@bptrust.org.uk **ⓛ** 13.00–17.00 Mon & Tues, Thur & Fri, 11.00–17.00 Sat & Sun, closed Wed **ⓝ** Central city bus service **ⓘ** Admission charge

Pump Room

Now used as a stylish breakfast, lunch and afternoon tea venue with background classical music provided by the famous Pump Room Trio, this striking building was built in the 18th century as a social facility next to the Roman Baths. For more than two centuries it was at the heart of Bath's social scene. It was here that wealthy residents would come to dance, listen to classical music and engage in conversation. Its lavish décor provides the setting for a memorable dining experience. You can drink the natural spring waters here too. **ⓐ** Stall Street **ⓣ** 01225 444477 **ⓦ** www.romanbaths.co.uk **ⓔ** romanbaths_bookings@ bathnes.gov.uk **ⓛ** 09.00–17.30 daily (summer); 09.00–16.30 daily (winter) **ⓝ** Central city bus service

Sally Lunn's Refreshment House and Museum

Housed in the oldest building in Bath, which dates from 1483, this delightful three-storey living museum and restaurant celebrates the life of Huguenot baker Solange Luyon, known as Sally Lunn. It was here that she invented her delicious light brioche-style bun, which she sold to the people of Bath around 300 years ago. You can see her original kitchen and an exhibition that tells her story. The restaurant has an innovative daytime menu that revolves around her bun, and a medieval-style dinner menu. ⓐ 4 North Parade Passage ① 01225 461634 ⓦ www.sallylunns.co.uk ⓔ jon@sallylunns.co.uk ① 10.00–18.00 daily ⓝ Central city bus service

RETAIL THERAPY

Guildhall Market Comprising around 30 outlets in a covered building near the Guildhall, this market sells most things from

◔ *Take in the stunning views in the Parade Gardens*

confectionery to household items, fashions and accessories to traditional crafts. ⓐ High Street ⓣ 01225 460808 ⓦ www.bathguildhallmarket.co.uk ⓔ info@bathguildhallmarket.co.uk ⓛ 08.00–17.30 Mon–Sat, closed Sun ⓝ Central city bus service

Milsom Quarter Its mix of designer fashion shops with names like Gucci and Karen Millan catching your eye has helped Milsom Street to be recognised as one of the best shopping streets in the country. The quarter also includes Milsom Place, New Bond Street, George Street, Queen Street, Broad Street and Green Street, all with their own great shops. ⓝ Central city bus service

SouthGate Shopping Centre Bath's newest shopping mall, the SouthGate has more than 55 shops, including major department stores that sit comfortably with high-street names like Boots and WH Smith. Cafés provide welcome breaks. ⓐ 12 Southgate Street ⓣ 01225 469061 ⓦ www.southgatebath.com ⓛ 09.00–18.00 Mon–Wed, Fri & Sat, 09.00–20.00 Thur, 11.00–17.00 Sun ⓝ Central city bus service

TAKING A BREAK

egg Café £ ❶ Bright, welcoming and family-friendly, the egg Café has a wide choice of sandwiches, snacks, cakes and fruit, along with beverages. Extended opening times on theatre nights. ⓐ Theatre Royal, Saw Close ⓣ 01225 448844 ⓦ www.theatreroyal.org.uk ⓛ 09.00–17.00 daily ⓝ Central city bus service

Real Italian Ice Cream Company £ ❷ Whether your favourite is strawberry, chocolate or pistachio, this family-run ice-cream parlour is sure to have it. There are dozens of flavours to choose from. ⓐ 17 York Street ❶ 01225 330121 ⓛ 10.00–17.30 daily Ⓝ Central city bus service

Café Retro, York Street ££ ❸ An informal café with a chic feel, the Café Retro serves light snacks, speciality coffees and cakes to the sounds of jazz and Latin music. ⓐ 18 York Street ❶ 01225 339347 ⓛ 09.00–17.00 Mon–Sat, closed Sun Ⓝ Central city bus service

Earl of Manvers ££ ❹ Cocktails and teriyaki, sushi and tempura platters are on the menu at this new lounge restaurant linked to the Second Bridge music venue. ⓐ 10 Manvers Street ❶ 01225 464451 Ⓦ www.secondbridge.co.uk ⓔ mail@secondbridge.co.uk ⓛ 17.00–23.00 daily Ⓝ Central city bus service

Gascoyne Place ££ ❺ Artfully presented dishes and desserts are sure to make your dining experience at this chic pub memorable. The snug makes a good venue for your pre-dinner drinks. ⓐ Saw Close ❶ 01225 445854 Ⓦ www.gascoyneplace.co.uk ⓔ info@gascoyneplace.co.uk ⓛ 11.30–23.00 daily Ⓝ Central city bus service

Green Park Brasserie & Bar ££ ❻ Housed in an old railway station building, this atmospheric eatery offers bistro-style food

and wine all served with a helping of live jazz every evening.
ⓐ Green Park Road ⓣ 01225 338565
ⓦ www.greenparkbrasserie.com ⓛ 10.30–23.00 daily
ⓝ Central city bus service

Live Arts Café ££ ❼ Doubling as an art display area, this lively café is in the Chapel Arts Centre. It serves vegetarian bistro-style snacks and cappuccinos. ⓐ Lower Borough Walls
ⓣ 01225 461700 ⓦ www.chapelarts.org ⓔ info@chapelarts.org
ⓛ 11.00–18.00 daily ⓝ Central city bus service

Jazz Café £££ ❽ With tables outside and waiters serving breakfast through to salads and daily specials, this café is usually full of diners. Jazz plays quietly in the background.
ⓐ Kingsmead Square ⓣ 01225 329002

⬤ Stop at the Pump Room for lunch or tea and sample Bath's therapeutic water

Ⓦ www.bathjazzcafe.co.uk Ⓛ 08.30–18.00 Mon–Sat, 10.30–16.00 Sun Ⓝ Central city bus service

Thai Balcony £££ ❾ Serving authentic Thai and Malaysian dishes with a luxurious twist, this elegant eatery has a dedicated following of local diners. It offers a takeaway service too. Ⓐ 1 Seven Dials Ⓣ 01225 444450 Ⓦ www.thai-balcony.co.uk Ⓛ 12.00–14.30 and 18.00–23.00 daily Ⓝ Central city bus service

The Vaults Restaurant £££ ❿ Enjoy a pre-performance Mediterranean-style dinner and a glass of fine wine at this restaurant inside the Theatre Royal. Ⓐ Saw Close Ⓣ 01225 442265 Ⓦ www.theatreroyal.org.uk Ⓔ enquiries@theatreroyal.org.uk Ⓛ Variable Ⓝ Central city bus service

AFTER DARK

Bath MiniBar ⓫ This sophisticated bar and eatery serves authentic tapas, quiches, desserts and the finest Spanish cavas and champagne. Ⓐ 1 John Street Ⓣ 01225 333323 Ⓦ www.bathminibar.com Ⓛ 12.00–15.00 and 17.00–20.30 Tues–Sat, closed Sun & Mon

Coeur de Lion ⓬ Bath's smallest pub, this historic 18th-century inn is an ideal stop for a glass of something strong and an informal meal. Traditional Sunday lunch is a speciality. Ⓐ 17 Northumberland Place Ⓣ 01225 463568 Ⓦ www.coeur-de-lion.co.uk Ⓛ 11.00–23.00 daily Ⓝ Central city bus service

Komedia Bath ⑬ If you love stand-up comedy then the award-winning Komedia Bath could be for you. Pre-show meals can be enjoyed at its River Cottage Canteen. ⓐ 22–23 Westgate Street ⓣ 0845 293 8480 ⓦ www.komedia.co.uk ⓔ info@komedia.co.uk ⓛ 18.00–01.00 daily club, 09.00–16.00 daily canteen ⓝ Central city bus service

Little Theatre Cinema ⑭ Stay in touch with the latest films from around the world at this Art-Deco-style cinema. It also has special screenings during the Bath Film Festival. ⓐ St Michael's Place ⓣ 01225 330817 ⓦ www.picturehouses.co.uk/cinema/The_Little ⓛ 13.00–22.00 daily ⓝ Central city bus service

🔺 *Head to Milsom Street for a spot of shopping*

Upper Town

Imposing 18th-century Georgian buildings, museums, fashionable restaurants, hotels and antique shops, as well as private homes, all surrounded by acres of parkland and richly planted gardens, characterise the elegant Upper Town district of the city.

SIGHTS & ATTRACTIONS

Assembly Rooms

Once regarded as Bath's newest and most fashionable meeting place, this collection of elegant rooms was used by members of the aristocracy in the 18th century for playing cards, dancing, listening to music and drinking tea. Today, it is used for functions and houses the famous Fashion Museum. Take a tour to see its lavish interior. ⓐ Bennett Street ① 01225 477785 ⓦ www.fashionmuseum.co.uk/assembly_rooms ① 10.30–17.00 daily (summer); 10.30–16.00 daily (winter) ⓝ Bus: 2, 6 ① Admission charge

Beckford's Tower

This imposing folly was built in 1827 for wealthy English novelist, art collector and politician William Beckford (1760–1844) as a study, library and private art gallery. Today, it is a museum where visitors can see Beckford's extensive collection of paintings, objets d'art and books. ⓐ Lansdown Road ① 01225 422212 ⓦ www.bath-preservation-trust.org.uk ⓔ admin@bptrust.org.uk ① 10.30–17.00 Sat, Sun and Bank Hol, closed Mon–Fri (Apr–Oct) ⓝ Bus: 2, 6 ① Admission charge

Botanical Gardens

Located in the Royal Victoria Gardens, this 3.5-hectare (9-acre) garden is one of the finest in the region. Created in 1887, it has a series of walks that pass by ancient rose gardens, huge trees and a rock garden. In one area stands a replica of a Roman temple used as an education facility and exhibition centre. It was originally the city's exhibit in the British Empire Exhibition held in London in 1924. The extension of a woodland area created from an adjacent disused quarry was unveiled on its centenary in 1987. ⓐ Weston Road ⓣ 01225 396386 ⓦ www.bathnes.gov.uk ⓛ 09.00–17.00 daily ⓝ Bus: 14, 17, 319, 332, 337, 339, X39

The Circus

Like the Royal Crescent, the Circus is a masterpiece of Georgian architecture and one of the city's 'must-see' sights. It is divided into three equal segments that form a circle separated by Brock Street, Bennett Street and Gay Street. On approach, the visitor sees a Georgian façade ahead whichever street is taken. Facing inwards, the houses are made of Bath stone and lavishly carved with alternating triglyphs and emblems, while in the centre is a garden with plane trees. ⓐ The Circus ⓝ Bus: 2, 6

Georgian Gardens

Excavation work in the 1980s revealed hidden flowerbeds, walls, terraces and paths that once formed part of the garden owned by a wealthy family who lived on this site. The garden has been restored, replanted with flowers and shrubs known to have grown here in the 19th century and is now a living museum showing how gardeners would have designed their outdoor spaces during this period. ⓐ Behind No 4 The Circus ⓘ 01225 477752 ⓒ 09.00–19.00 daily ⓝ Bus: 2, 6

Royal Crescent

This long, semicircular collection of 30 fine Georgian houses was designed by celebrated architect John Wood the Elder and his son, John Wood the Younger, and built between 1767 and 1775. It is considered an outstanding example of the architecture of the period and is Grade I listed. The crescent has remained almost unchanged since it was built and has provided the backdrop for countless films and television programmes set in Georgian times. One of the houses is now a hotel, while another is a museum, but most remain private homes.

ⓐ Royal Crescent ⓝ Bus: 2, 6

⬥ Plan a visit to No 1 Royal Crescent and admire the stunning architecture

Royal Victoria Park

Opened in 1830 by 11-year-old Princess Victoria, who would later become queen, this park was the first to carry her name. It is a beautiful park that was originally designed as an arboretum and has an impressive collection of mature trees. Lawns dotted with walkways spread over its 23 hectares (57 acres). Its leisure facilities include a boating lake, children's play area, tennis courts and a bowling green. **ⓐ** Marlborough Lane **ⓣ** 01225 394041 **ⓦ** www.bathnes.gov.uk **ⓛ** Daily **ⓝ** Bus: 14, 17, 319, 332, 337, 339, X39

CULTURE

Bath Aqua Theatre of Glass

Through a series of demonstrations, the team at this innovative working museum-cum-glassblowing studio shows how glass artists might have worked years ago to create stained-glass windows. They also demonstrate techniques used today to fashion glass jewellery, paperweights, ornamental sculptures and baubles. **ⓐ** 105–107 Walcot Street **ⓣ** 01225 428146 **ⓦ** www.bathaquaglass.com **ⓔ** studio@bathaquaglass.com **ⓛ** 09.30–17.00 Mon–Sat, closed Sun **ⓝ** Bus: 6, 7, 13, 231, 232, 271, 272, 273 **ⓘ** Admission charge

Building of Bath Museum

If, while gazing at the remarkable buildings of Bath, you begin to wonder just how the architects and builders created such a beautiful city, then a visit to this museum will explain all. Through a series of displays it tells how a building was constructed from the cellar upwards, what tools and materials were used and how the finishing decorative features were achieved. There is a scale model of the city as it was in Georgian times, and models of some of its buildings. The museum is housed in a Gothic chapel, which also holds the Bath Buildings Record. ⓐ The Countess of Huntingdon's Chapel, The Vineyards, The Paragon ⓣ 01225 333895 ⓦ www.bath-preservation-trust.org.uk ⓛ 10.30–17.00 Sat–Mon, closed Tues–Fri (summer) ⓝ Bus: 2, 6

Fashion Museum

This mesmerising museum was founded in the 1960s when a collection of costumes was donated to the city by fashion designer and historian Doris Langley Moore OBE (1902–89). It is now three times its original size, with displays of fashion dating from the 17th century right up to the present day. See its Dress of the Year collection with works by leading designers, including Mary Quant, Jean Muir, Giorgio Armani and Alexander McQueen. ⓐ Bennett Street ⓣ 01225 477173 ⓦ www.fashionmuseum.co.uk ⓔ fashion_bookings@bathnes.gov.uk ⓛ 10.30–17.00 daily (summer); 10.30–16.00 daily (winter) ⓝ Bus: 2, 6 ⓘ Admission charge

Jane Austen Centre

Celebrating the life of Jane Austen (1775–1817), a prolific novelist and author of romantic fiction classics such as *Sense and Sensibility*, published in 1811, *Pride and Prejudice* (1813) and *Emma* (1815), the centre is one of Bath's most popular visitor attractions. Housed in a Georgian building, it has rooms with displays showing how Jane might have lived. ⓐ 40 Gay Street

ⓘ 01225 443000 Ⓦ www.janeausten.co.uk
ⓔ contactus@janeausten.co.uk Ⓛ 09.45–17.30 daily (Apr–Oct,
until 19.00 Thur–Sat July & Aug); 11.00–16.30 Sun–Fri,
09.45–17.30 Sat (Nov–Mar) Ⓝ Bus: 2, 6 ⓘ Admission charge

Museum of Bath at Work
A reconstructed soft-drinks factory, engineering works, cabinet
maker's workshop and an ironmonger's shop are just some of
the authentic displays at this museum, which tells the story of
Bath's industrial heritage from Roman times to the present day.
One of the main exhibition areas explains the history of Bath

🔺 *Learn about Jane Austen's Bath experiences at The Jane Austen Centre*

stone, how it is quarried and used, and its impact on the city. You can take a guided tour or wander freely with an audio guide and interact with the displays. ⓐ Julian Street ⓣ 01225 318348 ⓦ www.bathatwork.co.uk ⓛ 10.30–17.00 daily (summer); 10.30–17.00 Sat & Sun, closed weekdays (winter); closed Dec ⓝ Bus: 2, 6 ⓘ Admission charge

Museum of East Asian Art

With displays of ceramics and metal decorative items, jades and bronzes from Japan, Korea and China, this museum gives a fascinating insight into oriental craftsmanship. The museum was founded in 1990 by Brian McElney, who retired to Bath after having lived in Asia all his working life and amassing a collection of around 2,000 objets d'art. Some of the collection's treasures are believed to date from the Stone Age.
ⓐ 12 Bennett Street ⓣ 01225 464640 ⓦ www.meaa.org.uk
ⓔ info@meaa.org.uk ⓛ 10.00–17.00 Tues–Sat, 12.00–17.00 Sun
ⓝ Bus: 2, 6 ⓘ Admission charge

No 1 Royal Crescent Museum

A former residence of the Duke of York, son of George III, this museum is the first house you come to when you approach Royal Crescent. It is cared for by the Bath Preservation Trust, which has skilfully decorated and furnished the house as it might have been when a wealthy family lived here in the 18th century. See its elegant drawing room and a gentleman's study. There is a bedroom decorated in the fashion of the day and a kitchen equipped with authentic pots and utensils.
ⓐ 1 Royal Crescent ⓣ 01225 428126 ⓕ 01225 481850

ⓦ www.bath-preservation-trust.org.uk ⏱ 10.30–17.00 Tues–Sun, closed Mon (summer); 10.30–16.00 Tues–Sun, closed Mon (winter) ⓝ Bus: 2, 6 ⓘ Admission charge

RETAIL THERAPY

Upper Town

If you are looking for antiques, collectible works of art or beautiful pieces of jewellery then head for the stylish specialist shops of the Upper Town area. Here you will also find top-quality designer fashion labels and exquisite evening wear in Saville Row, Margaret's Buildings and Bartlett Street.

Western Quarter

The Western Quarter lies south of the Upper Town area and comprises St James's Parade, Kingsmead Square and Green Park Station. Here, you will find a colourful mix of crafts, fresh flowers

● *Royal Victoria Park was opened by 11-year-old Princess Victoria in 1830* and food. The excellent Bath Farmers' Market is held at the station every Saturday. ⓐ Green Park Station ⓣ 01761 490624 ⓦ www.bathfarmersmarket.co.uk

TAKING A BREAK

Aqua Italia £ ⑮ Housed in a glorious arts and crafts building, this informal eatery serves tasty pizzas and garlic bread accompanied by great Italian wines inside or in its alfresco dining courtyard. ⓐ 88 Walcot Street ⓣ 01225 471371 ⓦ www.aqua-restaurant.com ⓔ bath@aqua-restaurant.com ⓛ 11.00–22.00 daily (until 22.30 Fri & Sat) ⓝ Bus: 6, 7, 13, 173, 231, 232, 271, 272

Hole in the Wall £ ⑯ The longest-established restaurant in Bath, this cosy eatery serves classic English à la carte dishes with a bistro-style twist. ⓐ 16–17 George Street ⓣ 01225 425242 ⓦ www.theholeinthewall.co.uk ⓔ info@theholeinthewall.co.uk ⓛ 12.00–15.00 & 18.00–22.00 Mon–Sat, 12.00–16.00 & 18.30–21.30 Sun ⓝ Bus: 2, 6, 7

Belvedere Wine Vaults ££ ⑰ This cosy pub-cum-restaurant venue serves both traditional pub food and à la carte cuisine, with a glass of beer or good wine. ⓐ Lansdown Road ⓣ 01225 330264 ⓛ 12.00–15.00 & 17.30–23.00 Mon–Sat, 12.00–15.00 & 18.00–22.30 Sun ⓝ Bus: 2

Hudson Steakhouse & Bar ££ ⑱ The finest farm-assured steaks, along with artfully presented seafood dishes and gourmet burgers, plus cocktails, are on the menu at this trendy steakhouse. ⓐ 14 London Street ⓣ 01225 332323 ⓦ www.hudsonbars.co.uk ⓛ 17.00–23.00 Mon–Sat, closed Sun ⓝ Bus: 7, 13

Jane Austen Centre Regency Tea Rooms ££ ⓳ Enjoy cakes and scones with a choice of 15 different types of loose tea or coffee at this charming tea room inside the Jane Austen Centre. ⓐ 40 Gay Street ⓣ 01225 443000 ⓦ www.janeausten.co.uk ⓔ contactus@janeausten.co.uk ⓛ 09.45–17.30 daily (Apr–Oct), until 19.00 Thur–Sat, July & Aug); 11.00–16.30 Sun–Fri, 09.45–17.30 Sat (Nov–Mar) ⓝ Bus: 2, 6

Beaujolais Bistro Bar ££–£££ ⓴ Try a dish from the à la carte menu or simply share an informal coffee with some friends at this lovely bistro bar. ⓐ Chapel Row, Queen Square ⓣ 01225 423417 ⓦ www.beaujolaisbath.co.uk ⓔ beaujolaisbath@hotmail.com ⓛ 11.00–23.00 Sun–Fri, 10.00–23.00 Sat ⓝ Bus: 2, 6

Aió Restaurant £££ ㉑ If you adore Mediterranean cuisine you will be spoilt for choice at this atmospheric eatery; everything from calamari, pasta and olives to Sardinian Fregola Sarda is on the menu. ⓐ 7 Edgar Buildings, George Street ⓣ 01225 443900 ⓦ www.aiorestaurant.co.uk ⓔ info@aiorestaurant.co.uk ⓛ 10.00–23.00 daily ⓝ Bus: 2, 6, 7

The Circus Café & Restaurant £££ ㉒ Breakfast and mid-morning coffee through to tasty lunches and evening cuisine, all made using mainly organic produce, are served at this fashionable eatery on the corner of the Circus. ⓐ 34 Brock Street ⓣ 01225 466020 ⓦ www.thecircuscafeandrestaurant.co.uk ⓛ 10.00–24.00 Mon–Sat, closed Sun Ⓝ Bus: 2, 6

Dower House Restaurant £££ ㉓ The elegant restaurant of the Royal Crescent Hotel, this eatery serves cuisine inspired by Europe and the Far East. Dine inside or alfresco in the garden, overlooking the manicured lawns. Children's menu also available. ⓐ 16 Royal Crescent ⓣ 01225 823333 ⓦ www.royalcrescent.co.uk ⓔ info@royalcrescent.co.uk ⓛ 12.30–14.00, 19.00–22.00 daily Ⓝ Bus: 2, 6

⬥ The ballroom in the Assembly Rooms is the largest Georgian interior in Bath

Olive Tree Restaurant £££ ❷ Whether choosing a fixed-price lunch or a full à la carte experience, the Olive Tree located within The Queensberry Hotel doesn't disappoint. ⓐ Russell Street ❶ 01225 447928 ⓦ www.thequeensberry.co.uk ⓔ reservations@thequeensberry.co.uk ⓛ 18.00–23.00 daily ⓝ Bus: 2, 6

AFTER DARK

Blathwayt Arms ❷ Combining a country-pub feel with quality cuisine accompanied by fine wines, this venue is ideal after a day at the races or for a pre-theatre meal. ⓐ Lansdown Road ❶ 01225 421995 ⓦ www.theblathwayt-bath.co.uk ⓛ 12.00–14.30 & 18.00–21.30 Mon–Fri, 12.00–21.30 Sat & Sun ⓝ Bus: 2

Star Inn ❷ Famous for its relaxed atmosphere where you can enjoy a glass of good ale, this pub housed in a 16th-century building has a dedicated following. Bar snacks are available. ⓐ 23 The Vineyards, The Paragon ❶ 01225 425072 ⓦ www.star-inn-bath.co.uk ⓔ landlord@star-inn-bath.co.uk ⓛ 12.00–14.30 & 17.30–23.00 Mon–Fri, 12.00–23.00 Sat, 12.00–22.30 Sun ⓝ Bus: 7, 13

Sub 13 ❷ This fashionable below-ground cocktail bar serves colourful creations, along with the finest wines – a great place to go for pre-theatre drinks. ⓐ 4 Edgar Buildings, George Street ❶ 01225 466667 ⓦ www.sub13.net ⓔ drinks@sub13.net ⓛ 17.00–24.00 Mon–Thur, 17.00–01.00 Fri, 17.00–01.30 Sat, closed Sun ⓝ Bus: 2, 6, 7

Pulteney Quarter

The charming Pulteney Quarter provides everything on the wish list for a great city stay, from admiring Georgian architecture to boating on the canal, picnicking in Henrietta Park or people-watching while enjoying lunch along the Grand Parade.

SIGHTS & ATTRACTIONS

Grand Parade

An attractive street of Georgian houses and shops, Grand Parade is one of the main thoroughfares on the approach to Pulteney Bridge. It lies alongside the River Avon overlooking the beautiful Parade Gardens, which are known for their floral displays. Here you can find the entrance to the Guildhall Market.
ⓐ Grand Parade ⓝ Central city bus service

Great Pulteney Street

Long, wide and imposing, this street is lined with properties dating from the 18th century. It links Pulteney Bridge with the Sydney Gardens and the Bathwick area. Commissioned by Sir William Pulteney, a Bath landowner and once said to be the country's wealthiest man, it is considered one of Bath's finest streets. ⓐ Great Pulteney Street ⓝ Bus: 8, 18, 264, 418, 419

Henrietta Park

A favourite place with locals as well as visitors, this park has richly planted flowerbeds, lawns and a pond, and can often be seen full of picnickers. It dates from 1897 when it opened to

🔺 *Laura Place*

celebrate Queen Victoria's Diamond Jubilee. One of its features is the King George V Memorial Garden, which was designed using plants chosen for their scent. Henrietta Street Bus: 8, 18, 264, 265, 418, 419

Kennet and Avon Canal

Stretching from Reading in Berkshire to the town of Keynsham near Bristol, this historic canal passes by Bath through Sydney Gardens to the east. You can enjoy cycling along the towpath or take a narrowboat trip along this stretch of water, including a ride on the Jubilee Narrowboat from Brassknocker Marina. The canal is also an important wildlife area. The Canal Centre, Brassknocker Marina 0800 121 4682 Bus: X4, X5

Laura Place

This attractive 18th-century square revolves around its central fountain. Originally the fountain was to have been a column fashioned like Nelson's Column in London, but residents objected. Today, it has a notable collection of listed buildings and lies between Pulteney Bridge and Great Pulteney Street. Laura Place Bus: 8, 18, 264, 265, 418, 419

Pulteney Bridge

One of the landmarks of Bath, this bridge spans the River Avon and was designed by neoclassical architect Robert Adams (1728–92) to echo the design of the Ponte Vecchio in Florence, Italy. It has the distinction of being one of only four bridges in the world to have shops built into the original 18th-century design. Pulteney Bridge Bus: 8, 18, 264, 265, 418, 419

The Kennet and Avon Canal lock gates

Sydney Gardens

Bath's oldest park, Sydney Gardens, was created by landscape architect Charles Harcourt Masters (1759–c.1820) in 1795. It is said to have been a favourite place of Jane Austen. Covering around 5 hectares (12 acres) in size, it features flowerbeds and mature trees, along with a period building housing the Holburne Museum. ⓐ Sydney Road ❶ 01225 394041 Ⓦ www.bathnes.gov.uk Ⓝ Bus: 8, 18, 264, 265, 418, 419

CULTURE

American Museum in Britain

Housed in a fabulous manor house, this museum takes the visitor through periods of American history from the time of the earliest settlers to the present day. It contains the finest collection of American artefacts outside the United States. ⓐ Claverton Manor, Claverton Down ❶ 01225 460503 Ⓦ www.americanmuseum.org ⓔ info@americanmuseum.org 🕒 12.00–17.00 Tues–Sun, closed Mon Ⓝ Bus: 8, 18, 418, 419 ❶ Admission charge

Holburne Museum of Art

An eclectic mix of paintings by Zoffany, Stubbs and Bath's own Thomas Gainsborough, furniture, porcelain and sculptures has long made this one of the finest art museums in the country. A major development programme, to be completed in 2011, will enhance its importance further. The museum is currently closed to the public until 2011. ⓐ Great Pulteney Street ❶ 01225 466669 Ⓦ www.bath.ac.uk ⓔ Holburne@bath.ac.uk Ⓝ Bus: 8, 18, 264, 265, 418, 419

Victoria Art Gallery

This superb art gallery has collections of paintings, sculptures and caricatures over several floors from the 15th century right through to the present day. Among the finest examples is the *Portrait of Sophia Dumergue* by Zoffany, dating from around 1780. ⓐ Bridge Street ⓣ 01225 477232 ⓦ www.victoriagal.org.uk ⓔ Victoria_enquiries@bathnes.gov.uk ⓛ 10.00–17.00 Tues–Sat, 13.30–17.00 Sun, closed Mon ⓝ Central city bus service

RETAIL THERAPY

Artisan Quarter

Comprising Walcot Street and London Street, the area of Bath that has become known as the Artisan Quarter is a mix of

▲ *There are both temporary and permanent exhibits at the Victoria Art Gallery*

small shops selling everything from paints and brushes for budding artists, paintings, fashions and textiles to antique furniture and clocks. Most of the shops are housed in period buildings, which provide the perfect backdrop to the colourful displays.

Podium Shopping Centre

High-street names sit alongside specialist shops in this bright and spacious shopping mall. Whether it's the latest fashion you are looking for, jewellery, cards or gifts, you are sure to find it here. Restaurants and cafés provide a place to stop for coffee or a meal. The town's library is also located inside the complex. ⓐ Northgate Street ⓣ 01225 444678 ⓦ www.thepodiumbath.co.uk ⓛ 08.00–23.00 Mon–Sat, 10.00–23.00 Sun ⓝ Central city bus service

TAKING A BREAK

Bath YMCA £ ㉘ More than just a gym and place to stay. Bright, modern and inexpensive, this informal dining restaurant serves breakfasts from early morning, snacks and light lunches. ⓐ Broad Street Place ⓣ 01225 325900 ⓦ www.bathymca.co.uk ⓛ 07.00–14.00 Mon–Fri, closed Sat & Sun ⓝ Central city bus service

Caffe Piazza £ ㉘ Located on the first floor of the Podium Shopping Centre, this lively informal eatery serves breakfast, lunch and dinner, including handmade pizzas and pasta with authentic sauces. The décor depicts scenes of Italy. ⓐ Northgate

Street ☎ 01225 429299 ⓦ www.caffepiazza.co.uk 🕒 07.30–23.00
Mon–Sat, 10.00–23.00 Sun Ⓝ Central city bus service

OPA £ ㉚ If you adore Greek cuisine then you will enjoy an
evening at the Greek-themed OPA. Dishes include gourmet-style
moussaka. Modern and fresh, this eatery lies beside the River
Avon. Ⓐ 14 North Parade ☎ 01225 317900 ⓦ www.opabath.com
🕒 11.30–23.00 Mon–Sat, closed Sun Ⓝ Bus: 4

Bathwick Boatman Restaurant ££ ㉛ Overlooking the River
Avon, this family restaurant offers the chance to enjoy dishes
from its European-inspired menu alfresco on its riverside
terrace. Ⓐ Forester Road ☎ 01225 428844
ⓦ www.bathwickboatman.com 🕒 12.00–15.00 and 18.00–23.00
Tues–Sat, 12.00–14.00 Sun, closed Mon Ⓝ Bus: 4

Café du Globe ££ ㉜ This popular restaurant is Bath's only
Moroccan-themed eatery. Its décor is traditional Moroccan,
while the menu features dishes such as meat and fish tagines
(stew) with couscous. Ⓐ 1A North Parade ☎ 01225 466437
ⓦ www.cafeduglobe.co.uk 🕒 10.00–23.00 Mon–Sat, 10.00–22.30
Sun Ⓝ Bus: 4

Rajpoot ££ ㉝ One of the city's longest-established Indian
restaurants, the Rajpoot has an atmospheric décor and an
extensive menu. Dishes are authentic à la carte Indian.
Ⓐ 4 Argyle Street ☎ 01225 466833 ⓦ www.rajpoot.com
🕒 12.00–14.30 daily, 18.00–23.00 Sun–Thur, 18.00–23.30 Fri & Sat
Ⓝ Bus: 8, 18, 264, 265, 418, 419

◆ *The River Avon with Pulteney Bridge in the background*

GG's Steak House & Grill £££ ㉞ Steaks cooked to perfection are the speciality of this stylish restaurant. It also serves fish dishes and desserts and offers an extensive wine list. ⓐ Spring Gardens Road ❶ 01225 311184 Ⓦ www.ggsteakhouse.co.uk ⓔ dine@ggsteakhouse.co.uk ❶ 12.00–15.00 and 18.30–24.00 Tues–Sun, closed Mon Ⓝ Bus: 8, 18, 264, 265, 418, 419

Onefishtwofish £££ ㉟ With catches delivered daily from the coast, this is one of the best fish and seafood restaurants in Bath. Its speciality is Bouillabaisse, plus it offers meat dishes and some fine wines. ⓐ 10 North Parade ❶ 01225 330236 Ⓦ www.onefishtwofishbath.co.uk ❶ 18.00–22.00 Tues–Sat, closed Sun & Mon Ⓝ Bus: 4

Tilleys Bistro £££ ㊱ Housed in a beautiful period property, this chic and welcoming bistro serves both English and French à la carte and lighter snack meat and fish dishes. It also has a good range of vegetarian dishes. ⓐ North Parade Passage ❶ 01225 484200 Ⓦ www.tilleysbistro.co.uk ❶ 12.00–14.30, 18.00–22.30 Mon–Sat, closed Sun Ⓝ Bus: 4

Vito's £££ ㊲ Serving dishes and wines that are authentic to the regions of Puglia in southern Italy, such as *capunti con zampina, funghi e pomodorini al filo* (pasta from Puglia with homemade sausage, oyster mushrooms, cherry tomatoes and chilli), this atmospheric restaurant is popular with locals. Food is freshly prepared. ⓐ 12 Argyle Street ❶ 01225 423481 Ⓦ www.vitosbath.co.uk ❶ 18.00–22.30 Mon–Sat, closed Sun Ⓝ Bus: 8, 18, 264, 265, 418, 419

AFTER DARK

Celsius Ice Bar 🕭 Housed in an underground vault, this unforgettable bar has been created to resemble a snow and ice cave. Temperatures inside are around −5°C (23°F). It serves a range of drinks. ⓐ 1 South Parade ☏ 01225 312800 ⓦ www.celsiusicebar.co.uk ⓔ info@celsiusicebar.co.uk ⏱ 18.00–23.00 daily Ⓝ Central city bus service

Lambrettas Bar 🕭 With a décor that takes its inspiration from the Lambretta Scooter, this fashionable bar offers wines and spirits, beers and snacks. ⓐ North Parade ☏ 01225 464650 ⏱ 11.30–23.00 Sun–Thur, 11.30–24.00 Fri & Sat Ⓝ Bus: 4

▶ *The cliffs of Cheddar Gorge*

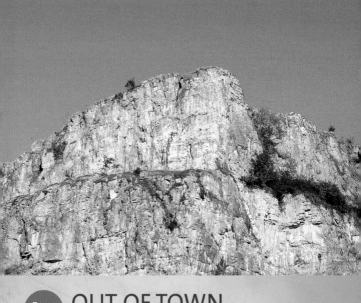

OUT OF TOWN

trips

Somerset

The county of Somerset is an ideal day-trip destination for all the family. The spectacular caves at Cheddar Gorge will appeal to all ages, while the beautiful cathedral city of Wells and the town of Radstock have their own historical appeal.

GETTING THERE

Head due south to reach the city of Wells, a journey of around 34 km (21 miles), along with the enchanting village of Cheddar, which is around 51 km (32 miles) away, and the conservation town of Radstock, 18 km (11 miles) away.

SIGHTS & ATTRACTIONS

Cheddar

See the dramatic stalactites and stalagmites in the caves of this village that has been inhabited since Neolithic times. A complete skeleton of a man who lived 9,000 years ago was discovered here in 1903. Cheddar Gorge is the largest gorge in the country and considered a Site of Special Scientific Interest.

Radstock

The town of Radstock is one of the country's best-preserved former coal-mining towns. A museum tells its history. Along with the neighbouring village of Midsomer Norton, Radstock is a popular excursion from Bath.

◆ *Wells Cathedral*

Wells

The smallest city in England after the City of London, Wells dates from medieval times and its quaint streets are a delight to explore. It was granted city status in 1205. Wells Cathedral dominates the skyline, along with the adjacent 13th-century Bishop's Palace.

CULTURE

Radstock Museum, Radstock

With a fascinating mix of displays that include a coal miner's cottage, a mine and coalface, machinery, a replica shop, Victorian classroom and wartime memorabilia, this museum is dedicated to coal mining. ⓐ Waterloo Road ⓣ 01761 437722 ⓦ www.radstockmuseum.co.uk ⓔ info@radstockmuseum.co.uk ⓛ 14.00–17.00 Tues–Fri, Sun and Bank Hol Mon, 11.00–17.00 Sat, closed Mon except Bank Hols, closed Dec and Jan ⓘ Admission charge

Wells Cathedral & Wells and Mendip Museum, Wells

Dating back to 1180, the present cathedral dominates the city and occupies the site of a church built in 705. See its Chapter House, Vicar's Hall and the fabulous cloisters. The city museum lies opposite and tells the fascinating story of the cathedral and its surroundings. Cathedral: ⓐ Cathedral Green ⓣ 01749 674483 ⓦ www.wellscathedral.org.uk ⓔ office@wellscathedral.uk.net ⓛ 10.00–17.00 Mon–Sat, 11.00–17.00 Sun. Museum: ⓐ Cathedral Green ⓣ 01749 673477 ⓦ www.wellsmuseum.org.uk ⓔ wellsmuseum@ukonline.co.uk ⓛ 11.00–17.00 daily (summer); 11.00–16.00 daily (winter) ⓘ Admission charge

RETAIL THERAPY

Wells City Centre

You will find everything from antiques, crafts and jewellery to fashions in the quaint shops that line the city's High Street. At the end of High Street is Well's picturesque and historic marketplace, where a market has been held for the past 800 years. Fill up on fresh produce every Wednesday and Saturday when it's market day.

TAKING A BREAK

Fromeway, Radstock £ A traditional country inn that was once the village butchery with its own slaughterhouse, the Fromeway offers a range of drinks as well as snacks like home-made soup and wholesome meals in its restaurant. ⓐ Frome Road
ⓣ 01761 432116 ⓦ www.fromeway.co.uk ⓛ 12.00–23.00 daily

Brufani's Grill Restaurant, Wells ££ This elegant restaurant within the landmark White Hart Hotel specialises in steaks and home-made gourmet-style burgers with innovative salads. There is a real log fire and children's menus are also available. ⓐ Sadler Street ⓣ 01749 672056 ⓦ www.whitehart-wells.co.uk
ⓛ 17.30–21.30 daily

Pickwicks Caffe, Wells ££ Combine viewing local artists' work with an informal meal of bistro-style sandwiches, snacks and salads. Pickwicks also serves breakfast. ⓐ Broad Street
ⓣ 01749 676697 ⓛ 07.30–17.30 daily

Cotswolds & Wiltshire

Bath borders the beautiful countryside of the Cotswolds and
Wiltshire, with towns, villages and attractions to discover, such
as Bradford on Avon, which is around 13 km (8 miles) away, and
historic Stonehenge, about 61 km (38 miles) away.

GETTING THERE

The Cotswolds lie due north of Bath, while Wiltshire lies to the
east. Both are easily reached via the A46.

SIGHTS & ATTRACTIONS

Bradford on Avon

This charming market town dates back centuries. With its
ancient bridge, a Saxon church, tithe barn and a museum with
displays of archaeological finds from the area, it makes a good
excursion from Bath. Ⓦ www.bradfordonavon.co.uk

Lacock

A National Trust village, medieval Lacock has some of the finest
half-timbered houses in the area. It was once a major wool town
and immensely prosperous. Ⓦ www.nationaltrust.org.uk

Longleat

With its famous lions and tigers in the safari park, along with a
stately home, a maze, boat rides and children's play area,
Longleat is a great family day out. ⓐ Longleat, Warminster

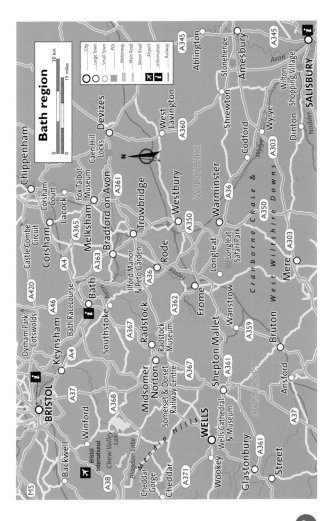

☎ 01985 844885 ⓦ www.longleat.co.uk
ⓔ enquiries@longleat.co.uk 🕓 10.00–16.00 (safari park), 10.00–
17.00 (Longleat House) daily, 17.00 safari park 17.30 Longleat
House on Sat & Sun, Bank Hols and school hols (summer)

Salisbury

A compact city with a mix of trendy restaurants and specialist
shops, Salisbury is a delight to explore. It is dominated by its
13th-century cathedral, which is considered the finest example
of early Gothic style in the country.

CULTURE

Caen Hill Locks, Devizes

The flight of 29 recently restored locks that cross the Kennet and
Avon Canal at Devizes is a spectacular sight. You can enjoy
waterside walks and the peaceful countryside here.

Dyrham Park, Dyrham

A National Trust property, this magnificent Baroque stately
home stands in over 100 hectares (250 acres). See its 17th-
century furnishings and spend some time exploring its park
trails. ⓐ Dyrham ☎ 0117 937 2501 ⓦ www.nationaltrust.org.uk
🕓 House 11.00–17.00 Mon & Tues, Fri–Sun, closed Wed & Thur
(summer); park 11.00–17.30 daily ❶ Admission charge

Ilford Manor & Peto Garden, Bradford on Avon

With its terraces, mature trees and views, this Italian-inspired
garden in the grounds of a historic manor house has won awards.

@ Bradford on Avon **①** 01225 863146 **Ⓦ** www.ilfordmanor.co.uk
@ info@ilfordmanor.co.uk **Ⓛ** 14.00–17.00 Tues–Thur, Sat & Sun,
closed Mon except Bank Hol & Fri (May–Sept); 14.00–17.00 Sun
& Easter Mon (Apr & Oct) **①** Admission charge

Stonehenge

Dating back to prehistoric times, this World Heritage Site gives
an insight into how ancient civilisations lived. **@** Near Salisbury
① 0870 333 1181 **Ⓦ** www.english-heritage.org.uk **Ⓛ** 09.00–19.00
daily (summer); 09.30–16.00 daily (winter) **①** Admission charge

RETAIL THERAPY

Salisbury City Centre

From designer fashions to crafts, the shops around Salisbury's
main thoroughfare are diverse and most are housed in medieval

⬥ *The stunning Cotswolds landscape*

half-timbered houses. Every Tuesday and Saturday the city hosts a bustling market.

TAKING A BREAK

Bernieres Tea Room, Salisbury £ A quintessential English tea room serving cream teas, snacks, cakes and coffee.
ⓐ 58 The Cathedral Close ⓣ 01722 413666 ⓛ 10.00–17.00 daily

Cellars Restaurant, Longleat ££ This bistro-style café can be found in the stately house at Longleat. ⓐ Longleat, Warminster
ⓣ 01985 844885 ⓦ www.longleat.co.uk
ⓔ enquiries@longleat.co.uk

The Sign of the Angel, Lacock ££ This 15th-century inn has English home cooking on the menu. ⓐ Church Street
ⓣ 01249 730230 ⓦ www.lacock.co.uk ⓔ angel@lacock.co.uk
ⓛ 07.30–22.00 daily

Tollgate Inn, Bradford on Avon £££ A traditional village inn with home-made dishes. ⓐ Ham Green ⓣ 01225 782326
ⓦ www.tollgateholt.co.uk ⓔ alison@tollgateholt.co.uk
ⓛ 11.30–22.00 daily

ⓞ *Bath Tourist Information Centre*

PRACTICAL
information

Directory

GETTING THERE

Bath is easy to reach via the road, rail and air network.
By road it is best approached by using the M4 motorway from
London and Wales, leaving at Junction 18, and via the M5
motorway from Devon and Cornwall. National Express
(ⓦ www.nationalexpress.com) coaches operate from London
Victoria coach station and from London Heathrow and London
Gatwick airports. Journey times average around two and a half
hours. Rail travellers will arrive into Bath Spa station, which is
located off Dorchester Street near the new SouthGate Shopping
Centre. Trains arrive here direct from London Paddington station
and London Waterloo station (journey time around 90 minutes)
and from Cardiff Central, Frome, Portsmouth Harbour,
Gloucester, Southampton and Brighton, and trains from
other destinations via Bristol Temple Meads station.
Air travellers will arrive into **Bristol International Airport**
(ⓦ www.bristolairport.co.uk), which is around 32 km (20 miles)
from Bath, or from London's Heathrow Airport
(ⓦ www.heathrowairport.com) and Gatwick Airport
(ⓦ www.gatwickairport.com), which are around 160 km
(100 miles) and 225 km (140 miles) from Bath, respectively.

Many people are aware that air travel emits CO_2, which
contributes to climate change. You may be interested in
the possibility of lessening the environmental impact
of your flight through the charity **Climate Care**
(ⓦ www.jpmorganclimatecare.com), which offsets your CO_2
by funding environmental projects around the world.

GETTING AROUND

One of the best ways to get around is on foot. The city centre, Upper Town and the Pulteney Quarter are easy to navigate, but be sure to have a good map with you. A central city bus service links all the major sights; it is operated by the First Group (☎ 01224 650100 🌐 www.firstgroup.com). Buses leave from the bus station on Dorchester Street opposite Bath Spa train station. A route map and timetable are available from the station's information point. There are bus routes for travelling further afield, including service 2 that goes to Lansdown Road, services 1 and 13 that serve Combe Down, service 264/265 for Bradford on Avon, and for the cathedral city of Wells service 173. If planning a visit to Lacock village, take service 231/233 and for Bristol service X39. Bath has many taxi companies for long or short journeys. The main taxi ranks are outside Bath Spa train station and Westgate Buildings, next to Bath Abbey.

Enterprise Rent-A-Car ⓐ Lower Bristol Road ☎ 01225 443311
🌐 www.enterprise.co.uk Ⓝ Bus: 5, 8, 10, 418, 419

Europcar ⓐ Brassmill Lane ☎ 0176 147 9205
🌐 www.europcar.co.uk Ⓝ Bus: 337, 339, 418, X39

Hinton Garage ⓐ Albion Place ☎ 01225 422131
🌐 www.hintongarage.co.uk ✉ info@hintonvauxhall.co.uk
Ⓝ Bus: 14, 17, 319, 332, 337, 339, X39

HEALTH, SAFETY & CRIME

The crime rate in Bath is on a parallel with most other cities in England; in a busy place with lots of people, crime does occasionally occur. You should exercise vigilance to avoid becoming the victim of pickpockets or having your vehicle

broken into. Dial 999 for any emergency. The police station is located in Manvers Street, a short distance from Bath Spa station.

OPENING HOURS

Most attractions open around 10.00–17.00, although some stay open later. Offices and shops tend to open from 09.00 until 17.30, although the larger shopping malls stay open well into the evening. Banks are generally open from 09.00 to 15.30. Markets vary but are usually open from 08.00 through to around midday, although some remain open until 17.30.

TOILETS

Bath has good provision of public toilets. Find them near the Podium Shopping Centre, at the Riverside Coach Park in Avon Street, in Charlotte Street off Queen Square and in the Royal Victoria Park near Gravel Walk, plus inside the attractions, shopping malls and restaurants.

CHILDREN

Bath is particularly child-friendly and most of the attractions have reduced admission rates for children. Restaurants have child menus and most of the parks have playgrounds for children to enjoy.

TRAVELLERS WITH DISABILITIES

Bath welcomes people with a disability and aims to provide facilities that enable them to get about easily and see the sights. The city operates a Shopmobility scheme whereby wheelchairs or scooters are available for hire (ⓐ 7–9 Lower Borough Walk ☎ 01225 481744 ⓦ www.bathnes.gov.uk), and there are designated car parking areas for disabled drivers in most of the city's car parks. Bath Tourism and most of the attractions provide ramps as well as guides for visitors with impaired hearing or vision.

FURTHER INFORMATION

The Bath Tourist Information Centre can be found at Abbey Chambers in the Abbey Churchyard. ☎ 0906 711 2000 ⓦ www.visitbath.co.uk ⓔ tourism@bathtourism.co.uk

WHAT'S ON INFORMATION

To find out what's on, visit the Bath Tourism website ⓦ www.visitbath.co.uk/whats-on. Other websites for independent listings include ⓦ www.whatsonbath.co.uk and ⓦ www.bath.co.uk. Entertainment information is printed in newspapers and magazines, including the *Bath Chronicle*. ⓦ www.thisisbath.co.uk

ACKNOWLEDGEMENTS

The photographs in this book were taken by Zenna West for
Thomas Cook Publishing, to whom the copyright belongs, except for
the following:
Bath and Northeast Somerset Council page 7; Bath Thermae Spa
page 13 (Andy Short); Shutterstock pages 11, 39, 71, 79, 81, 87

Project editor: Jennifer Jahn
Copy editor: Cath Senker
Proofreaders: Jan McCann & Rosemary Moore
Layout: Donna Pedley
Indexer: Marie Lorimer

AUTHOR BIOGRAPHY

Carole French is an award-winning BBC-trained journalist with a passion
for architecture. With its Georgian and Roman heritage, Bath has always
been one of her favourite cities. A member of the British Guild of Travel
Writers and a property expert, Carole divides her time between homes
in the UK and the Mediterranean.

Send your thoughts to
books@thomascook.com

- Found a great bar, club, shop or must-see sight that we don't feature?

- Like to tip us off about any information that needs a little updating?

- Want to tell us what you love about this handy little guidebook and
  more importantly how we can make it even handier?

Then here's your chance to tell all! Send us ideas, discoveries and
recommendations today and then look out for your valuable input
in the next edition of this title.

Email the above address (stating the title) or write to:
pocket guides Series Editor, Thomas Cook Publishing, PO Box 227,
Coningsby Road, Peterborough PE3 8SB, UK.